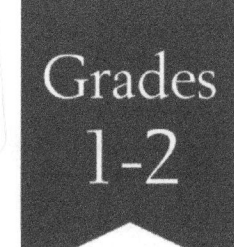

Grades 1-2

PRINCESS
WRITING WORKBOOK
PRINTING PRACTICE STORYBOOK WITH PARAGRAPHS

- Princess Writing Workbook
    Printing Practice Storybook with Paragraphs
- Copyright © 2014 by Engage-N-Learn™
    All rights are reserved.

Engage-N-Learn grants educators and parents or guardians the right to photocopy activity pages from this workbook for non-commercial classroom or personal instruction. Except as already noted, no portion of this workbook may be copied, reproduced, stored, or transmitted by any means (including, but not restricted to, electronic, photocopying, recording), without the express written consent of the publisher, Engage-N-Learn.

www.engagenlearn.com

- Written by staff at Engage-N-Learn
    www.engagenlearn.com
- Cover design by Melissa Stevens
    www.theillustratedauthor.net
- Interior illustrations by Melissa Stevens
    www.theillustratedauthor.net
- Formatting by Chris McMullen
    www.chrismcmullen.com

ISBN-13: 978-1-941691-00-7

Children's > Educational > Handwriting

Contents

- Introduction — v
- Uppercase Alphabet — vi
- Lowercase Alphabet — vii
- Interactive Questions — viii
- Story #1: A Dream Come True — 9
- Reading Questions for Story #1 — 60
- Story #2: The Princess Game — 65
- Reading Questions for Story #2 — 119
- Answers to Assessment Questions — 124

Engage-N-Learn™

Our mission is to engage students in learning fundamental skills through creative, yet purposeful and effective, activities.

www.engagenlearn.com

Practice printing letters, words, phrases, sentences, and stories:
- *Princess Writing Workbook* series
- *Sports Writing Workbook* series

Practice writing cursive letters, words, phrases, sentences, and stories:
- *Fairy Handwriting Workbook* series
- *Space Handwriting Workbook* series

Learn and practice adding, subtracting, multiplying, and dividing:
- *Pirates Arithmetic Workbook* series
- *Fashion Arithmetic Workbook* series

Learn and practice fractions skills:
- *Yucky Bugs! Fractions Workbook*
- *So Pretty! Fractions Workbook*

Look for new workbooks coming soon.
Find free learning resources at engagenlearn.com.

Introduction

This *Princess Writing Workbook* series offers more than writing practice: It also features a princess theme to help engage students in learning. The page design includes a decorative border and the writing relates to princesses.

This volume of the series, *Printing Practice Storybook with Paragraphs*, includes the following features:
- Tracing the letters of words in sentences.
- Copying sentences onto blank lines.
- Standard three lines to help write correctly.
- Two complete stories related to princesses.
- Reading comprehension questions after each story.
- Alphabet pages review how to write each letter.

Here are some suggestions for how to use this workbook:
- Make learning a positive experience through praise, encouragement, and support.
- Do one page at a time. Take periodic breaks. Work in a quiet environment.
- Interact with the child by asking questions about the story. Inspect the written work every few pages.
- Strive to make the process fun and engaging.

Uppercase Alphabet

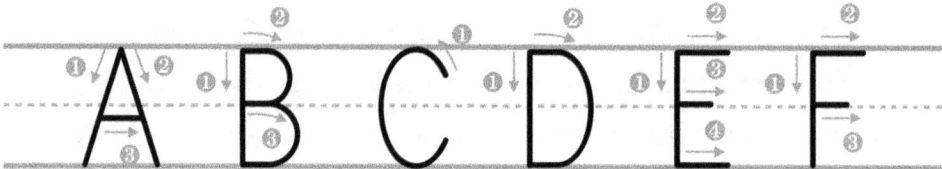
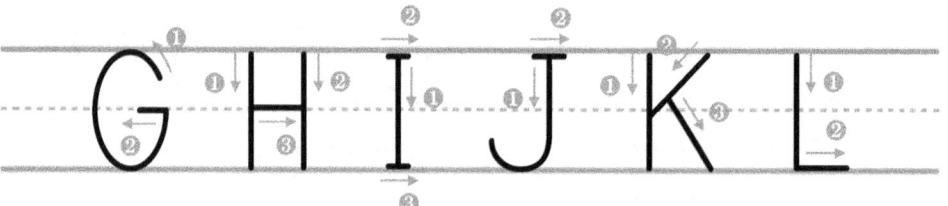
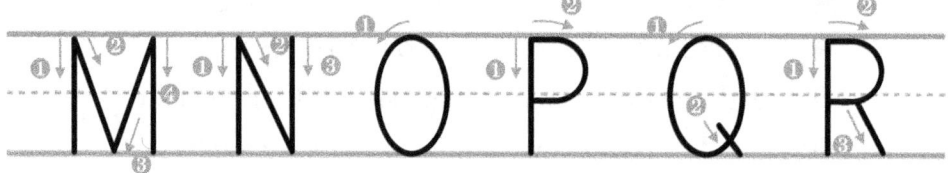
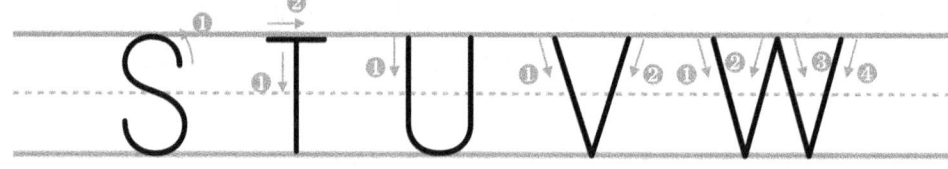
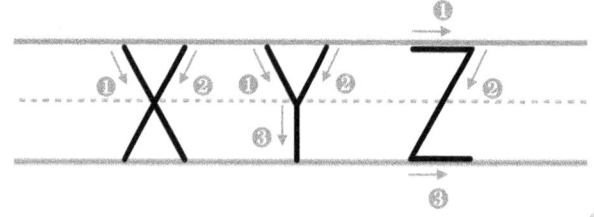

Lowercase Alphabet

a b c d e f

g h i j k l

m n o p q r

s t u v w

x y z

Interactive Questions

One way to help make learning a fun and engaging process is through positive interactions. The sample questions that follow can be used to help engage children in the activities:

Basic
- Ask if the child enjoys the border design.
- Read a page aloud. Show your interest.
- Have the child identify simple, common words.
- Encourage the child to ask what a word means.
- Ask simple questions that can build confidence.
- Let the child draw a related picture on blank paper.

Intermediate
- Ask the child to read a page aloud.
- Close the book and ask the child to spell a word.
- See if the child knows what a word means.

Advanced
- Have the child complete the reading questions.
- Ask occasional questions that challenge the child.
- Have the child tell you about the story after reading.
- Let the child write a related story on blank paper.

Story #1

A Dream Come True

Name: _____

Trace and write.

Once upon a time

there lived a sweet

girl named (print your name here).

She dreamed about

being a princess.

Princess Writing Workbook: Printing Practice Storybook with Paragraphs

Name: _____

Trace and write.

One day, (print your name here)

looked up at the sky

and saw a beautiful

rainbow made of

bright colors.

Princess Writing Workbook: Printing Practice Storybook with Paragraphs

Name: _____

Trace and write.

(print your name here) wondered if

there really is a pot

of gold at the end of

the rainbow. She

decided to find out.

Princess Writing Workbook: Printing Practice Storybook with Paragraphs

Name: _____

Trace and write.

It was a wonderful

day to go for a walk.

(print your name here) wondered how

long it would take to

reach the rainbow.

Name: _____

Trace and write.

During her walk,

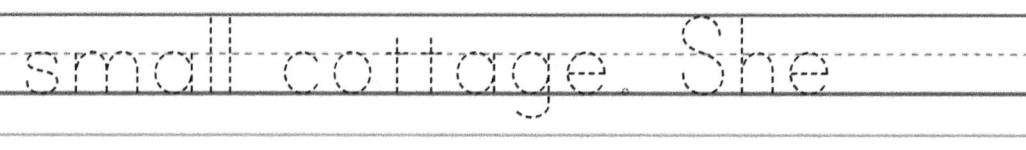
(print your name here) came to a

small cottage. She

didn't remember

seeing it before.

Princess Writing Workbook: Printing Practice Storybook with Paragraphs

Name: _____

Trace and write.

It was even smaller

than her playhouse.

The door was so tiny

that (print your name here) couldn't

fit through it.

Princess Writing Workbook: Printing Practice Storybook with Paragraphs

Name: _____

Trace and write.

(print your name here) wondered who

lived there, but didn't

stop to find out. She

wanted to reach the

rainbow soon.

Princess Writing Workbook: Printing Practice Storybook with Paragraphs

Name: _____

Trace and write.

Beyond the cottage

was a garden.

There were many

colorful flowers and

pretty butterflies.

Princess Writing Workbook: Printing Practice Storybook with Paragraphs

Name: _____

Trace and write.

(print your name here) heard bells

ringing. It sounded

like the bells were

coming from the

rainbow.

Princess Writing Workbook: Printing Practice Storybook with Paragraphs

Name: _____

Trace and write.

As (print your name here) got closer

to the rainbow, the

ringing became louder.

She reached the end

of the rainbow.

Name: _____

Trace and write.

A cute fairy with

sparkly wings hovered

above a pot of gold.

(print your name here) couldn't

believe her eyes!

Princess Writing Workbook: Printing Practice Storybook with Paragraphs

Name: _____

Trace and write.

The fairy wore a tiny

tiara made out of

flowers. They looked

just like the flowers

back at the cottage.

Name: _____

Trace and write.

The fairy asked

(print your name here) if she would

like to make a wish.

Of course, she would!

What a silly question!

Princess Writing Workbook: Printing Practice Storybook with Paragraphs

Name: _____

Trace and write.

(print your name here) told the fairy

that she has always

dreamed about being

a princess. Could her

dream come true?

Princess Writing Workbook: Printing Practice Storybook with Paragraphs

Name: _____

Trace and write.

The fairy told (print your name here)

to look into the pot.

When (print your name here) looked

into it, she saw that

it wasn't full of gold.

Princess Writing Workbook: Printing Practice Storybook with Paragraphs

Name: _____

Trace and write.

It was filled with

specks of glittery

fairy dust. It looked

like millions of tiny

sparkly diamonds.

Princess Writing Workbook: Printing Practice Storybook with Paragraphs

Name: _____

Trace and write.

The fairy explained

that the fairy dust is

magical. If (print your name here)

makes a wish, her

wish will come true.

Princess Writing Workbook: Printing Practice Storybook with Paragraphs

Name: _____

Trace and write.

(print your name here) closed her

eyes and made a

wish while the fairy

sprinkled the dust

over (print your name here)'s head.

Princess Writing Workbook: Printing Practice Storybook with Paragraphs

Name: _____

Trace and write.

Poof! (print your name here) turned

into a real princess.

The fairy held up a

mirror so that (print your name here)

could see herself.

Princess Writing Workbook: Printing Practice Storybook with Paragraphs

Name: _____

Trace and write.

(print your name here) saw a very

beautiful princess in

the mirror. She was

wearing a fancy blue

dress and shiny tiara.

Princess Writing Workbook: Printing Practice Storybook with Paragraphs

Name: _____

Trace and write.

Wow! (print your name here) was

very excited. This was

the best day of her

life! It really was a

dream come true!

Princess Writing Workbook: Printing Practice Storybook with Paragraphs

Name: _____

Trace and write.

Suddenly, a horse

pulled an elegant

carriage to where

(print your name here) and the fairy

were standing.

Princess Writing Workbook: Printing Practice Storybook with Paragraphs

Name: _____

Trace and write.

The horse had a

braided mane and

there were flowers

woven into the

braids.

Princess Writing Workbook: Printing Practice Storybook with Paragraphs

Name: _____

Trace and write.

(print your name here) stepped into

the carriage and

waved goodbye. She

rode the carriage to

a large castle.

Name: _____

Trace and write.

Outside the castle

were colorful flowers

and green shrubs in

the shapes of many

kinds of animals.

Princess Writing Workbook: Printing Practice Storybook with Paragraphs

Name: _____

Trace and write.

When they reached

the moat, the

drawbridge lowered.

A prince stood just

outside the doors.

Name: _____

Trace and write.

When the prince saw

(print your name here), he came over

to help her out of the

carriage. Then he

invited her inside.

Name: _____

Trace and write.

The prince gave

(print your name here) a tour of the

castle. (print your name here) had her

own room since she

was now a princess.

Princess Writing Workbook: Printing Practice Storybook with Paragraphs

Name: _____

Trace and write.

(print your name here)'s room had

a large walk-in closet

with hundreds of

gowns, dresses,

shoes, and jewels.

Princess Writing Workbook: Printing Practice Storybook with Paragraphs

Name: _____

Trace and write.

(print your name here) even had her

own vanity room

where she could get

dressed, do her hair,

and put make-up on.

Princess Writing Workbook: Printing Practice Storybook with Paragraphs

Name: _____

Trace and write.

All of the clothes

looked very elegant.

(print your name here) was asked to

get dressed for the

royal ball.

Princess Writing Workbook: Printing Practice Storybook with Paragraphs

Name: _____

Trace and write.

(print your name here) couldn't decide

which dress to wear.

She closed her eyes,

spun in a circle, and

grabbed a dress.

Princess Writing Workbook: Printing Practice Storybook with Paragraphs

Name: _____

Trace and write.

When (print your name here) was

dressed and ready

for the ball, she

walked over to the

sitting room.

Princess Writing Workbook: Printing Practice Storybook with Paragraphs

Name: _____

Trace and write.

The prince told (print your name here)

how beautiful she

looked. He grabbed

her hand and led her

to the ballroom.

Princess Writing Workbook: Printing Practice Storybook with Paragraphs

Name: _____

Trace and write.

(print your name here) spent the night

singing and dancing

with the prince. She

smiled all the time.

It was very exciting!

Princess Writing Workbook: Printing Practice Storybook with Paragraphs

Name: _____

Trace and write.

There was a table

filled with cookies

and cakes. (print your name here)

could eat anything

she wanted. Yummy!

Princess Writing Workbook: Printing Practice Storybook with Paragraphs

Name: _____

Trace and write.

(print your name here) didn't have a

bedtime. She could

eat and dance all

night long. She danced

as long as she could.

Princess Writing Workbook: Printing Practice Storybook with Paragraphs

Name: _____

Trace and write.

When (print your name here) finally

became sleepy, she

returned to her room,

sat on her bed, and

looked around.

Name: _____

Trace and write.

Everything was very

pretty. Yet (print your name here)

felt sad. But why?

She should be the

happiest girl on earth!

Princess Writing Workbook: Printing Practice Storybook with Paragraphs

Name: _____

Trace and write.

What was wrong with

her? (print your name here)'s dream

had come true. She

lived at the castle

with a kind prince.

Princess Writing Workbook: Printing Practice Storybook with Paragraphs

Name: _____

Trace and write.

(print your name here) realized that

the castle didn't have

everything. She really

missed her family

and friends.

Princess Writing Workbook: Printing Practice Storybook with Paragraphs

50

Name: _____

Trace and write.

Being a princess

didn't make (print your name here)

happy. Living in a

castle didn't make

her happy either.

Princess Writing Workbook: Printing Practice Storybook with Paragraphs

Name: _____

Trace and write.

(print your name here) had everything

she needed to be

happy at her home.

She wanted to see

family and friends.

Princess Writing Workbook: Printing Practice Storybook with Paragraphs

Name: _____

Trace and write.

Now (print your name here) had a

tummy ache from all

of the sweets she

ate. She started

crying.

Princess Writing Workbook: Printing Practice Storybook with Paragraphs

Name: _____

Trace and write.

Someone gently shook

(print your name here). She opened

her eyes and saw her

mother and father

looking at her.

Princess Writing Workbook: Printing Practice Storybook with Paragraphs

Name: _____

Trace and write.

Her parents told

(print your name here) that she was

okay. She looked

around. She was back

in her old bedroom.

Princess Writing Workbook: Printing Practice Storybook with Paragraphs

Name: _____

Trace and write.

(print your name here) was happy to

be home in her old

bed with her favorite

teddy bear. Had it all

just been a dream?

Princess Writing Workbook: Printing Practice Storybook with Paragraphs

Name: _____

Trace and write.

(print your name here)'s father leaned

over and kissed her

on her forehead. Then

he said, "Goodnight,

my little princess."

Princess Writing Workbook: Printing Practice Storybook with Paragraphs

Name: _____

Trace and write.

(print your name here) fell asleep with

a smile on her face.

She is her daddy's

princess. That's the

best kind of princess!

Princess Writing Workbook: Printing Practice Storybook with Paragraphs

Name: _____

Trace and write.

They lived happily

ever after. It was

a very happy ending

for a sweet little

princess.

Princess Writing Workbook: Printing Practice Storybook with Paragraphs

Reading Questions for Story #1

Name: _____

Instructions: Write a short answer to each question below. Parents or teachers can find the answers on pages 125-8.

1. Who do you think lived in the small cottage?

2. What sound was coming from the rainbow?

3. Who did the girl meet when she reached the end of the rainbow?

Princess Writing Workbook: Printing Practice Storybook with Paragraphs

Name: _____

4. What did the girl wish for when she reached the end of the rainbow?

5. What was the pot of gold filled with?

6. How did the princess go to the castle?

7. Who met the princess at the castle?

Princess Writing Workbook: Printing Practice Storybook with Paragraphs

Name: _____

8. Why was the princess sad?

9. How did the princess get a tummy ache?

10. Where did the princess want to go?

11. Did the girl's wish really come true?

Princess Writing Workbook: Printing Practice Storybook with Paragraphs

Name: _____

12. Describe what you would do if you could be a prince or princess for a day.

Story #2

The Princess Game

Name: _____

Trace and write.

Anna loves to play

video games. She is

very good at them.

Her favorite game is

about a princess.

Princess Writing Workbook: Printing Practice Storybook with Paragraphs

Name: _____

Trace and write.

If Anna's mom didn't

limit the time she

can play the games,

she would play them

all day long.

Princess Writing Workbook: Printing Practice Storybook with Paragraphs

Name: _____

Trace and write.

Anna's dad joked,

"If you don't stop

playing these games,

you will become a

part of one."

Princess Writing Workbook: Printing Practice Storybook with Paragraphs

Name: _____

Trace and write.

Anna's favorite

character is Princess

Haley. Anna tries to

help Princess Haley

return to her castle.

Princess Writing Workbook: Printing Practice Storybook with Paragraphs

Name: _____

Trace and write.

Every night when

Anna goes to sleep,

she dreams about

finally unlocking the

door to the castle.

Princess Writing Workbook: Printing Practice Storybook with Paragraphs

Name: _____

Trace and write.

One morning, when

Anna woke up, she

was no longer Anna.

She had turned into

Princess Haley. Oh my!

Princess Writing Workbook: Printing Practice Storybook with Paragraphs

Name: _____

Trace and write.

Anna's dad was right.

She was part of the

game, instead of just

playing it. Now the

game was real.

Princess Writing Workbook: Printing Practice Storybook with Paragraphs

Name: _____

Trace and write.

Anna found herself

in the Enchanted

Forest. That is the

first level of the

video game.

Princess Writing Workbook: Printing Practice Storybook with Paragraphs

Name: _____

Trace and write.

Anna was traveling

through the forest.

She was watching out

for dangers and

trying to score points.

Princess Writing Workbook: Printing Practice Storybook with Paragraphs

Name: _____

Trace and write.

The forest was dark

and spooky. Anna had

to leap over goblins

and duck beneath

bats. It wasn't easy!

Princess Writing Workbook: Printing Practice Storybook with Paragraphs

Copyright © Engage-N-Learn

Name: _____

Trace and write.

It didn't get easier

when Anna reached

the end of the forest.

A scary witch was

waiting for her.

Princess Writing Workbook: Printing Practice Storybook with Paragraphs

Name: _____

Trace and write.

Anna knew that her

magic wand didn't

have enough power

to make it past the

witch. Oh no!

Princess Writing Workbook: Printing Practice Storybook with Paragraphs

Name: _____

Trace and write.

Anna decided to run

back into the forest.

She knew that there

was a secret tunnel

in the forest.

Princess Writing Workbook: Printing Practice Storybook with Paragraphs

Name: _____

Trace and write.

The witch followed

Anna into the forest.

Anna ran quickly. This

made it even harder

to avoid the dangers.

Princess Writing Workbook: Printing Practice Storybook with Paragraphs

Name: _____

Trace and write.

A couple of times, a

goblin or bat almost

got Anna. Another

time, the witch nearly

caught up to her.

Name: _____

Trace and write.

Then Anna went even

faster and turned off

the path. Whew! The

witch didn't know

which way she went.

Princess Writing Workbook: Printing Practice Storybook with Paragraphs

Name: _____

Trace and write.

Anna found the entry

door to the tunnel.

She used her magic

wand to open the

heavy door.

Princess Writing Workbook: Printing Practice Storybook with Paragraphs

Name: _____

Trace and write.

Just as Anna was
entering the tunnel,
the witch appeared.
Anna shut the door as
fast as she could.

Princess Writing Workbook: Printing Practice Storybook with Paragraphs

Name: _____

Trace and write.

At the end of the

tunnel were three

doors. Anna picked

the left door, hoping

the witch would not.

Princess Writing Workbook: Printing Practice Storybook with Paragraphs

Name: _____

Trace and write.

Beyond the left door

was a slide that took

Anna to the Candy

Valley. Everything was

made out of candy.

Princess Writing Workbook: Printing Practice Storybook with Paragraphs

Name: _____

Trace and write.

The flowers and

trees were made of

chocolate. The grass

was made from jelly

beans. Yummy!

Princess Writing Workbook: Printing Practice Storybook with Paragraphs

Name: _____

Trace and write.

Not everything in

Candy Valley was

sweet, though. Anna

needed to watch out

for the giant ants.

Princess Writing Workbook: Printing Practice Storybook with Paragraphs

Name: _____

Trace and write.

The giant ants always

chase Princess Haley.

Anna knew the trick.

She picked several

leaves from the trees.

Princess Writing Workbook: Printing Practice Storybook with Paragraphs

Name: _____

Trace and write.

When a giant ant

appeared, Anna gave

it a leaf to eat. The

giant ant would be

busy eating the leaf.

Name: _____

Trace and write.

Anna needed to reach the candy store in order to go to the next level. She was running out of leaves.

Princess Writing Workbook: Printing Practice Storybook with Paragraphs

Name: _____

Trace and write.

There were too many

giant ants between

Anna and the candy

store. Oh, no! How

would she pass them?

Princess Writing Workbook: Printing Practice Storybook with Paragraphs

Name: _____

Trace and write.

Anna used her magic wand to turn the giant ants into tiny ants. She then ran to the candy store.

Princess Writing Workbook: Printing Practice Storybook with Paragraphs

Name: _____

Trace and write.

Anna recharged her

magic wand at the

candy store. Then she

boarded a train. This

was a chance to rest.

Princess Writing Workbook: Printing Practice Storybook with Paragraphs

Name: _____

Trace and write.

The train took Anna

to the Flower Garden.

The flowers not only

looked pretty, but

smelled nice, too.

Princess Writing Workbook: Printing Practice Storybook with Paragraphs

Name: _____

Trace and write.

A beautiful fairy met

Anna at the entrance

to the garden. The

fairy would help her

through the garden.

Name: _____

Trace and write.

Anna and the fairy

would pick flowers.

They are worth points

and can be traded to

charge the wand.

Princess Writing Workbook: Printing Practice Storybook with Paragraphs

Name: _____

Trace and write.

They must find a gold

flower in order to

advance to the next

level. It wasn't as

easy as it seems.

Princess Writing Workbook: Printing Practice Storybook with Paragraphs

Name: _____

Trace and write.

The roses have thorns

that reach out and

grab you if you make

too much noise. They

had to be very quiet.

Princess Writing Workbook: Printing Practice Storybook with Paragraphs

Name: _____

Trace and write.

Anna wanted to talk

to the fairy, but they

had to be quiet. They

picked a lot of pretty

flowers.

Princess Writing Workbook: Printing Practice Storybook with Paragraphs

Name: _____

Trace and write.

The fairy found the

gold flower. When

Anna picked it, she

was carried to the

Beauty Salon.

Princess Writing Workbook: Printing Practice Storybook with Paragraphs

Name: _____

Trace and write.

Princess Haley always

stops at the Beauty

Salon before going

to the castle. She has

to look like a princess!

Princess Writing Workbook: Printing Practice Storybook with Paragraphs

Name: _____

Trace and write.

Anna got her hair and

nails done. She also

went shopping for a

pretty dress. It wasn't

all fun, though.

Princess Writing Workbook: Printing Practice Storybook with Paragraphs

Name: _____

Trace and write.

The witch is always

disguised in the

Beauty Salon. Anna

needed to watch out

for her.

Princess Writing Workbook: Printing Practice Storybook with Paragraphs

Name: _____

Trace and write.

When Anna was all
ready, she admired
herself in the mirror.
She looked like an
elegant princess.

Princess Writing Workbook: Printing Practice Storybook with Paragraphs

Name: _____

Trace and write.

Suddenly, the witch

appeared on the

other side of the

mirror. Oh, no! Anna

was in danger.

Princess Writing Workbook: Printing Practice Storybook with Paragraphs

Name: _____

Trace and write.

It's a good thing that

Anna's wand was

fully charged. She

cast a magic spell

at the mirror.

Princess Writing Workbook: Printing Practice Storybook with Paragraphs

Name: _____

Trace and write.

Just then, the witch

cast an evil spell

toward Anna. It was

scary, but Anna's

spell reached first.

Princess Writing Workbook: Printing Practice Storybook with Paragraphs

Name: _____

Trace and write.

The mirror turned into

cement, sealing the

witch behind the

mirror. The witch was

trapped.

Princess Writing Workbook: Printing Practice Storybook with Paragraphs

Name: _____

Trace and write.

Anna called for her

fairy godmother and

went outside. A horse

appeared pulling a

beautiful carriage.

Princess Writing Workbook: Printing Practice Storybook with Paragraphs

Name: _____

Trace and write.

The horse-drawn carriage took Anna to the castle. The castle was large. The prince was waiting outside.

Name: _____

Trace and write.

When Anna stepped

out of the carriage,

he bowed down and

kissed her lightly on

her fingertips.

Princess Writing Workbook: Printing Practice Storybook with Paragraphs

Name: _____

Trace and write.

Anna, who was

Princess Haley, and

the prince went to the

bonus level. It's called

Happily Ever After.

Princess Writing Workbook: Printing Practice Storybook with Paragraphs

Name: _____

Trace and write.

Anna heard a voice.

"Anna, where are

you?" It was Anna's

mom. Suddenly, Anna

was back at home.

Princess Writing Workbook: Printing Practice Storybook with Paragraphs

Name: _____

Trace and write.

"I'm in my room,

replied Anna. "I was

playing my favorite

video game, the one

with Princess Haley."

Princess Writing Workbook: Printing Practice Storybook with Paragraphs

Name: _____

Trace and write.

"You're not going to

believe this. I was

there. I was a part

of the game. I was

Princess Haley!"

Princess Writing Workbook: Printing Practice Storybook with Paragraphs

Name: _____

Trace and write.

Anna said, "I finished every level. I went to the castle and met the prince. He kissed my fingertips."

Princess Writing Workbook: Printing Practice Storybook with Paragraphs

Name: _____

Trace and write.

"I will never wash my

hands," continued

Anna. "We found a

bonus level called

Happily Ever After."

Name: _____

Trace and write.

"I can't wait to play

my next game! Maybe

I can be in another

game. I had so much

fun! Wow!"

Princess Writing Workbook: Printing Practice Storybook with Paragraphs

Reading Questions for Story #2

Name: _____

Instructions: Write a short answer to each question below. Parents or teachers can find the answers on pages 125-8.

1. What did Anna spend too much time doing?

2. What did Anna's dad say would happen to her?

3. Who did Anna turn into?

Princess Writing Workbook: Printing Practice Storybook with Paragraphs

Name: _____

4. Where did Anna need to go in order to win the game?

5. What dangers did Anna need to watch out for in the forest?

6. Who was waiting for Anna as she was leaving the forest?

Princess Writing Workbook: Printing Practice Storybook with Paragraphs

Name: _____

7. How did Anna make it past the giant ants?

8. What did Anna do in order to trap the witch?

9. Does Anna want to become part of a video game again?

Princess Writing Workbook: Printing Practice Storybook with Paragraphs

Name: _____

10. Describe what it would be like to be part of your favorite video game.

Answers to Assessment Questions

Story #1

A Dream Come True

1. the fairy

2. bells ringing

3. a fairy

4. to turn into a princess

5. specks of glittery fairy dust

Princess Writing Workbook: Printing Practice Storybook with Paragraphs

6. a horse-drawn carriage

7. a prince

8. she missed her family and friends

9. she ate too many sweets

10. back home

11. no, it was just a dream

Story #2
The Princess Game

1. playing video games

2. she would become part of a game

3. Princess Haley

4. the castle

5. goblins and bats

Princess Writing Workbook: Printing Practice Storybook with Paragraphs

6. a mean witch

7. she used her magic wand to turn them into tiny ants (she also fed them leaves to keep them busy)

8. turned the mirror into cement

9. yes, she thought it was fun

Engage-N-Learn Books

Handwriting skill levels:
- Pre-letter lines, curves, and shapes skills (pre-K & up)
- Printing letters, numbers, and shapes (pre-K & up)
- Printing words, phrases, and sentences (grade K & up)
- Printing storybook with paragraphs (grades 1-2 & up)
- Pre-cursive forms and letters (grade 2 & up)
- Cursive letters and words (grade 2 & up)
- Cursive words, phrases, and sentences (grade 2 & up)
- Copying and rewriting cursive sentences (grade 3 & up)
- Cursive storybook with paragraphs (grade 3 & up)

Series and subjects:
- *Princess Writing* (Printing)
- *Sports Writing* (Printing)
- *Fairy Handwriting* (Cursive)
- *Space Handwriting* (Cursive)
- *Pirates Arithmetic*
- *Fashion Arithmetic*
- *Yucky Bugs! Fractions*
- *So Pretty! Fractions*

Look for new workbooks coming soon.
Find free learning resources on our website:

www.engagenlearn.com

Certificate of Achievement

This award certifies that

_____

(Write name above.)

exhibited the grace of a princess during these efforts to master the art of handwriting.

_____

(Date)